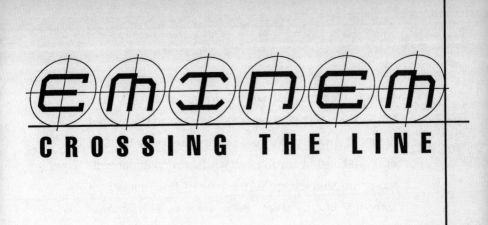

EMINEM
CROSSING THE LINE

MARTIN HUXLEY

ST. MARTIN'S GRIFFIN   NEW YORK

www.stmartins.com

Design by Heidi E. Eriksen

Library of Congress Cataloging-in-Publication Data

Huxley, Martin.
    Eminem : crossing the line / Martin Huxley.
      p. cm.
    ISBN 0-312-26732-0
    1. Eminem (Musician) 2. Rap musicians—
    United States—Biography. I. Title.
ML420.E56H89 2000
78214216.549'092—dc21
    [B]   00-040244

10 9 8 7 6 5 4 3

Sometimes I'm real cool,
but sometimes I could be a real asshole.
I think everyone is like that.

—EMINEM

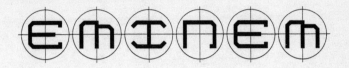

INTRODUCTION

"God sent me to piss the world off," Eminem boasts on his breakthrough hit "My Name Is." Considering the outpouring of press and public outrage that has accompanied the young white Detroit rapper's runaway success, that grandiose claim isn't hard to swallow.

As the new century dawns and the divisions between black and white youth culture continue to blur, this gleefully warped, inventively vulgar verbal acrobat has established himself as America's fastest-rising— and least likely—musical outlaw. Unlike most turn-of-the-millennium music stars, the bleach-blond, blue-eyed Eminem, nee Marshall Bruce Mathers III, is not just a charismatic pop idol. He's also a disturbingly unique artist who has won the sometimes grudging respect of hardcore hip-hop purists and critics as well as that of MTV-addicted white teens, thanks to his distinctively unhinged vocal delivery, his inventive rhyming skills and his appealingly warped lyrical persona.

But the adoring kids who know Eminem only through MTV's extensive exposure of the cleaned-up version of "My Name Is"—which depicts him as a lovably naughty bad boy—are only getting a small part of the story. His multiplatinum major-label debut, *The Slim Shady LP*, presents a much darker, psychologically complex character who resides in a considerably more frightening and nihilistic universe.

Eminem's vividly twisted rhymes embody a timely collision of Midwestern white trash and urban hip-hop cultures, while portraying an unpredictably violent yet oddly hilarious world seemingly bereft of hope or redemption. His lyrics convey a seething, barely contained rage that's channeled through the imagery of comic-book science fiction and gory slasher flicks into elaborately wacky but unmistakably personal revenge fantasies.

On *The Slim Shady LP*, the artist adopts the cartoonish yet unsettling persona of Slim Shady, spinning colorfully absurd narratives involving brutal violence, rough sex and imaginative sadism. Despite their wacky humor, Eminem's mischievously nasty scenarios reflect an all-encompassing sense of bitterness and hostility that reflects the tortured psyche of a deeply conflicted character whose real-life pain lurks beneath the surface of his outrageous alter ego. It's those contradictions that make Eminem a uniquely compelling artist, one whose appeal transcends boundaries of race and musical genre.

Though he's sometimes described as an overnight success, Eminem—who was just twenty-four years old when _The Slim Shady LP_ went platinum—spent nearly a decade honing his rhyming skills, building a reputation as one of the finest freestyle rappers in the Midwest prior to his ascent to mainstream stardom.

While certain details of his past are disputed by some witnesses, the established facts make it clear that the childhood of Marshall Bruce Mathers III was no bed of roses. Indeed, his turbulent youth was a seemingly endless series of soul-crushing hard knocks that would shape his personality in strange and unexpected ways.

Eminem's rebellious, contradiction-laden character was forged through such early challenges as the desertion of an absentee father, conflicts with a mother whom he now portrays as an emotionally unstable drug user, and numerous encounters with neighborhood violence.

Marshall Bruce Mathers III was born in Kansas City, Missouri, on October 17, 1975. He says that his mother, Debbie, was only fifteen when she and his father were married; his father, Marshall II, was seven years older. When Marshall III was born two years later, both parents were members of Daddy Warbucks, a cover band that worked in hotel lounges around the Dakota-Montana border.

Marshall II left the family six months after his son's birth and moved to California. Eminem has still never met him.

As a teen, Marshall would try sending letters to his dad, which were returned, unopened. But, in time-honored showbiz fashion, Em's father would eventually come out of the woodwork to attempt a reconciliation once his son had become famous.

The fatherless boy's self-described "stereotypical, trailer park, white trash upbringing" gave him an early taste of what it's like to be an outsider. He spent his early years shuttling with his mother between Missouri and Michigan, living with various relatives.

"We just kept moving back and forth because my mother never had a job," he now says. "We kept getting kicked out of every house we were in. I believe six months was the longest we ever lived in a house.

"I was born in Kansas City. I moved to Detroit when I was five. From five to nine, I lived in Kansas City again. We moved back for five years. Then we moved to Detroit permanently."

Changing schools frequently made it difficult for Marshall to form attachments and make friends. He became increasingly sensitive and introverted, retreating into comic books and television. "I didn't really start opening up until eighth grade, going into ninth."

The insecurities engendered by his unsettled home life were further fueled by frequent encounters with neighborhood gangs and local bullies. One of the most harrowing of these incidents later inspired him to write "Brain Damage," which namechecks D'Angelo Bailey, a grade-school classmate who administered a savage assault that left the future star in the hospital with a near-fatal cerebral hemorrhage.

The beating that nearly robbed the world of Slim Shady occurred at lunchtime recess one winter afternoon in 1983 while Marshall was in the fourth grade. After Marshall hassled a friend of Bailey's, Bailey "came running from across the yard and hit me so hard into this snowbank that I blacked out." The disoriented youngster was sent home from school. After his ear started bleeding, he was sent to the hospital, where he was diagnosed with a cerebral hemorrhage and spent much of the next ten days in a coma.

The alienated kid tapped into a much-needed source of personal validation and emotional release when he discovered rap music. He now says that his passion for hip-hop was sparked at the age of nine, at the moment he heard the Ice-T track

"Reckless," from the soundtrack album of the eighties breakdancing-exploitation flick *Breakin'*.

He quickly became a devoted convert to the still-emerging new genre, eagerly absorbing the inventively boisterous verbal outbursts of such groundbreaking artists as Run-DMC, the Beastie Boys and LL Cool J. "From LL to the Fat Boys, and all that shit, I was fascinated," he says. "When LL first came out with 'I'm Bad,' I wanted to do it, to rhyme. Standing in front of the mirror, I wanted to be like LL."

Marshall had received the *Breakin'* album from his uncle, Ronnie Polkinghorn, his mother's kid brother and an avid hip-hop fan. Though Ronnie was just a few months older than Marshall, he became a crucial influence on him, particularly when Ronnie began making primitive home recordings of his own raps.

When Ronnie committed suicide in 1993, Marshall was devastated.

In 1987, Marshall, his mom and his half-brother Nathan (who was born in 1986) returned to Michigan for good, settling in a poor, predominantly black neighborhood on the east side of Detroit.

Growing up in an economically disadvantaged area brought Marshall face-to-face with the randomness of urban violence, much of which carried racial undertones.

Attending Lincoln High School in Warren, Michigan, the troubled teen found solace from his bleak everyday existence—and found a much-needed source of self-esteem—in rap. He began writing and recording his own raps at the age of thirteen, and his budding rhyme abilities boosted his confidence, helping him to come out of his shell and make new friends. Adopting the stage name Eminem from his alliterative initials, Marshall would regularly compete in lunch-hour rhyme jousts, stacking up his already-impressive freestyling skills against those of his classmates.

At fifteen, Em formed his first rap group, Bassmint Productions. Two years later, he dropped out of high school after failing the ninth grade three times in a row. "I don't think it was necessarily 'cause I'm stupid," he says. "I didn't go to school. I couldn't deal."

He soon became immersed in Detroit's

local rap scene, putting together home-made cassettes of his rhymes and hustling them around town. He and a close pal, a young black MC named Proof, would compete at Saturday-night open-mike freestyle contests at the Hip-Hop Shop on Detroit's West 7 Mile, the epicenter of the local rap community. "As soon as I grabbed the mike, I'd get booed," he later recalled. "Once the motherfuckers heard me rhyme, though, they shut up."

Early on, Em's talents were noticed by Marky and Jeff Bass, a pair of Detroit hip-hop producers collectively known as the Funky Bass Team, or FBT Productions for short. The duo first heard the teenage Eminem on a late-night radio show on influential local station WHYT, and were so impressed that they called him at the station and invited him to record at their studio.

Eminem also paid some early dues performing with such local groups as Champtown, the New Jacks and Soul Intent. The latter act, a duo with DJ Buttafingas, released a single, "Fucking Backstabber"/"Biterphobia," in 1996. Em subsequently launched an all-star rap crew, the Dirty

Dozen (aka D-12), with Proof and four other locally prominent rappers.

While attempting to make his mark musically, Em drifted through a series of frustrating minimum-wage jobs, including an extended stint at Gilbert's Lounge, a family restaurant in suburban St. Clair Shores. But his real goals were never far from his mind.

"I like to throw my ideas just scattered onto paper," he told *The Source*. "When I was busing tables I'd write 'em on my hand or on receipts. I wrote rhymes on the wall in my old house right above my bed. I did it in pencil but one time when I went to wipe it off, it wiped off the paint. My mom fuckin' flipped."

On Christmas Day of 1995, Em's longtime girlfriend Kim Scott gave birth to the couple's daughter, Hailie Jade. His new parenthood motivated him to get more serious about pursuing his musical career. "I wanted to be a father to her, and not do what my father did to me. When Hailie was born, it was kind of a wake-up call to me. It was like, I have to do this shit, and really get up and go for it."

In the Fall of 1996, Eminem released his first solo album, *Infinite*, on the local Web Entertainment label. Though he had hoped that it would win him the respect of the local rap community, the disc received a less-than-rapturous response in Detroit (though the track "Searchin'" did receive some airplay on local urban station WCHB) and gained little national attention.

In hindsight, it's not hard to see why the album was unsuccessful. While the embryonic effort did show off Em's oral and lyrical abilities to some degree, it gives little indication of the explosive personality and audacious point of view that would later emerge, with little of the distinctive humor, twisted imagery and pent-up rage that would distinguish his subsequent work.

Infinite's rhymes are considerably tamer than the over-the-top spectacles for which the artist would subsequently become famous. Here, he mainly seems to be emulating other artists' styles rather than developing a distinctive voice of his own. The sparse backing tracks, meanwhile, feature a derivative stripped-down sound that's augmented by occasional horn or keyboard samples, as opposed to the fat grooves and imaginitive soundscapes that would emerge on *The Slim Shady LP*.

Eminem now insists he never liked *Infinite* much himself, acknowledging that his own personality got lost amidst his attempts to impress others rather than create something that honestly reflected his own personality.

"*Infinite* was me trying to figure out how I wanted my rap style to be, how I wanted to sound on the mic and present myself. It was a growing stage. I felt like

Infinite was like a demo that just got pressed up."

He further stated, "It was right before my daughter was born, so having a future for her was all I talked about. It was way hip-hopped out, like Nas and AZ—that rhyme style that was real in at the time. I've always been a smart-ass comedian, and that's why it wasn't a good album."

Still, the album, which featured production work from D-12 member Denine Porter, wasn't without its bright spots, some of which did hint, if only vaguely, at the promise which Eminem would ultimately fulfill.

The artist's early experiences with violence were reflected in the autobiographical "It's OK," while Em's ongoing economic struggles are addressed on "Never 2 Far," and the exuberant "Open Mic" captures the competitive chaos of the Saturday-night rap battles of Em's formative days at the Hip-Hop Shop. "Maxine" was a graphic narrative of an abortive sexual encounter with the unhinged title female, starting with a randy phone conversation and culminating with an unexpected twist when the eponymous character reveals that she has AIDS.

Elsewhere, the tongue-in-cheek urban nightmare "Backstabber" previews some of the cartoon anarchy that would later become Eminem's lyrical trademark, exaggerating an unpleasant personal experience into a distinctively extreme mini-epic.

Meanwhile, "W.E.G.O." showcased the talents of his sidekicks Proof and DJ Head, both of whom would continue to play prominent roles in Eminem's work in the future.

Though *Infinite* was lacking in the distinctive qualities that would emerge in his future work, Eminem's technical skills and lyrical craftsmanship were prominent enough to be noticed by journalist Marc Kempf, who would later serve as the artist's publicist. In an *Underground Soundz* review of *Infinite*, Kempf noted, "One of Em's tightest skills [is] his ability to hit back to back. [Rather than] rhyme the last syllable, Eminem will instead rhyme the last six syllables . . . His mastery of the English language allows him to write coherent stories, not just freestyle ramblings that happen to rhyme."

But such positive feedback was rare at the time, and this period proved to be a decidedly painful and frustrating one for Eminem. *Infinite*'s failure to click seemed to set in motion a long and agonizing downward spiral in his personal and professional life. This bleak period reached its low point when he was fired from his job at Gilbert's Lounge, leaving him broke and desperate just days before his daughter's first birthday.

Still, despite the hard times that followed *Infinite*'s release—and the insecurities that the album's lack of success fed—Eminem continued to work to promote the disc, doing live shows and radio performances, as well as participating in numerous freestyle competitions across the country. His perseverance gradually paid off, creating the beginnings of a buzz that extended beyond the boundaries of the Detroit scene. One tangible indication of Em's higher profile was a featured spot in *The Source*'s influential "Unsigned Hype" column.

If *Infinite*'s general failure proved anything to Eminem, it was that he wasn't likely to get much career mileage out of sounding like everyone else. It was obvious that he needed to figure out how to be himself on record if he was going to have any success.

Meanwhile, his worsening personal and financial situation, combined with his growing anger and bitterness over the scornful response that *Infinite* had received locally, became an unlikely source of inspiration for the troubled MC.

The hurt and resentment that he felt

eventually manifested itself in the form of Slim Shady, a semifictional character who would come to embody all of Eminem's nastiest thoughts and most extreme revenge fantasies. Appropriately enough, Em swears that inspiration struck while he was sitting on the toilet.

"I was takin' a shit," he told *The Source.* "I swear to God. And the fuckin' name just popped into my head. Then I started thinkin' of twenty million things that rhymed with it. Everybody in my clique had an alias. They was like, 'You can't just be Eminem. You gotta be Eminem aka somebody else.'"

Slim Shady quickly emerged as Eminem's lyrical alter ego, a mischievous antisuperhero whose principal mission was to inflict violence and humiliation on Marshall Mathers' real and imagined enemies, from the bullies who'd tormented him as a kid to the local scenesters who'd rejected *Infinite.*

"Slim Shady is just the evil thoughts that come into my head. Things I shouldn't be thinkin' about. Not to be gimmicky, but people should be able to determine when I'm serious and when I'm fuckin' around.

That's why a lot of my songs are funny. I got a warped sense of humor, I guess."

The wickedly colorful new character made his debut on the EP that bore his name, recorded in the spring of 1997. It was released independently the following year, but initially shopped around by Web Entertainment in the hope of getting Eminem a deal with a larger label possessing the industry clout to break him nationally.

The ten-track *Slim Shady EP*, produced by Em's longtime FBT admirers Mark and Jeff Bass, was a substantial improvement over its predecessor, dispensing with *Infinite*'s restrained approach in favor of a new, more confrontational persona and a more distinctive sound. Eminem's new raps also included several vitriolic references to various members of the Detroit hip-hop community, including some jabs at the local radio stations that had rejected *Infinite*.

The EP's standout tracks included the original versions of future *Slim Shady LP* highlights "Just Don't Give a Fuck" and "If I Had"—both of which reappear at the end of the disc in toned-down, radio-friendly alternate versions—along with

"Just the 2 of Us," an early version of the scandalous number that would later be re-worked as " '97 Bonnie and Clyde" on the album. Elsewhere, Em's family issues came to the fore on "Mommy," while his D-12 cohorts Bizarre and Swift made guest appearances on "No One's Iller."

The new material's scathing subject matter wasn't *The Slim Shady EP*'s only significant advance. The disc also spot-lighted a heightened level of songcraft, underlining Eminem's uncanny ability to merge vivid lyrics and tight beats into concise, cohesive songs, incorporating memorable choruses and melodic hooks while maintaining a distinctly complex, in-ventive rhyme structure.

The Slim Shady EP carried the unmis-takable vibe of a scrappy, hungry artist seizing the moment and rising to the oc-casion. "I had nothing to lose, but some-thing to gain," Em later noted. "If I made an album for me and it was to my satis-faction, then I succeeded. If I didn't, then my producers were going to give up on the whole rap thing we were doing. I made some shit that I wanted to hear. *The*

Slim Shady EP, I lashed out on everybody who talked shit about me."

The original cover of the demo version of *The Slim Shady EP* was a close-up shot of the artist's posterior, intended, no doubt, as a response to those who'd rejected his last recording effort. The cover art was later changed to the more familiar image of Em smashing a mirror.

"I had this whole Slim Shady concept of being two different people, having two different sides of me," he explained. "One of them I was trying to let go and I looked at the mirror and smashed it. That was the whole intro of *The Slim Shady EP*. Slim Shady was coming to haunt me, was coming to haunt Eminem."

The Slim Shady EP was recorded while Eminem was still living in desperate poverty in one of Detroit's most crack-infested, burglary-ridden neighborhoods with girlfriend Kim and Hailie. There, the fledgling family was on the receiving end of several burglaries, losing several TVs and VCRs and various pieces of furniture to local villains. In one apartment, a stray bullet flew through the kitchen window while Kim was washing dishes; fortunately, no one was hurt.

At one point, after being evicted from one apartment, Kim left Em, taking Hailie with her. "She's looking at me like, 'You're supposed to be the man, you're supposed to be taking care of your family and you can't even feed your fuckin' self,' " he later recalled in an MTV interview.

While his personal and economic circumstances continued to test his resolve, the time and energy that Eminem had invested in getting out and promoting himself was beginning to show some results. He'd given a copy of *Infinite* to the Rap Coalition's Wendy Day, who liked it enough to help him get a spot at the Coalition's 1997 Rap Olympics in Los Angeles, a high-profile annual MC competition that had the potential for gaining him substantial exposure.

The night before he was to fly west to participate in the Rap Olympics, Em came home to the apartment he was sharing with friends to find the locks changed and an eviction notice on the door. Since he had nowhere else to go, he broke into the now-vacant apartment, slept on the floor, woke up the next morning and headed for the airport.

Despite that rocky start, the LA trip proved to be a very productive one. While Em took second prize (out of fifty competing MCs) in the Rap Olympics' freestyle competition, he and his manager/lawyer, Paul Rosenberg, distributed copies of the *Slim Shady EP* demo to various music-industry insiders, including some Interscope Records staffers.

Em also got some major mileage out of an appearance on Sway and Tech's influential *Wake Up Show*, on the LA radio station 92.3 The Beat, on which he delivered some furious freestyling that caught the ear of several West Coast music-biz players—and which would later earn him the honor of being named the *Wake Up Show*'s 1997 Freestyle Performer of the Year.

His ability to rise to the occasion for that radio performance reflected the sense of urgency that gripped Eminem at a time when the future of his career—and his life—appeared to be in serious jeopardy. "I felt it's my time to shine," he says. "I have to rip this. At that time, I felt that it was a life or death situation."

4

Among those who were impressed with Eminem's performance on Sway and Tech's show was West Coast rap legend Dr. Dre. The former N.W.A. founder turned influential solo artist, producer and label entrepreneur had recently split from Suge Knight, his partner in the successful but controversial (and legally embattled) Death Row Records. At the time, Dre was in the process of launching a new imprint, Aftermath, distributed by the clout-heavy Interscope, home of such provocative acts as Tupac Shakur, Nine Inch Nails and Marilyn Manson.

Impressed by Em's performance on Sway and Tech's show, Dre remembered having seen a demo copy of *The Slim Shady EP* at Interscope's offices. After tracking down a copy, he immediately judged the relatively unknown young MC to be an excellent candidate for his new imprint's artist roster.

"Not too many people can turn me on off the first listen, without a visual," Dre said of his first exposure to *The Slim Shady EP*. "His [stuff] was complete. I could tell he spent time on his lyrics and that he was a perfectionist with how he delivered them."

Eminem, still smarting from the rejection he'd received in his previous attempt at making a mark on the hip-hop world, was deeply flattered by the praise of one of rap's most respected and influential figures, providing a much-needed boost to his battered self-esteem.

"It was an honor to hear the words out of Dre's mouth that he liked my shit," he said, adding, "Growing up, I was one of the biggest fans of N.W.A., from putting on the sunglasses and looking in the mirror and lip-synching, to wanting to be Dr. Dre, to be Ice Cube. This is the biggest hip-hop producer ever.

"I appreciate that he's basically putting his credibility on the line for me," he added. "Because if I come out wack, it could destroy his career."

Dr. Dre later told the *Los Angeles Times* that the issue of race was irrelevant in his interest in signing Eminem. "If you're dope, you're dope," he said. "When I got [*The Slim Shady EP*], I didn't know he was white. I didn't know he was white until the next day. And that didn't change jack.

"Actually," he admitted, "I looked at it as an edge. I really think that we're going to be able to get away with [lyrical] stuff that we wouldn't normally be able to get away with."

Dre's recognition, and the series of events that his interest set in motion, brought an end to the extended period of personal difficulty that had surrounded Em. Life had grown so bleak that, he would later reveal, he had even harbored thoughts of committing suicide, an issue which he'd alluded to in "My Name Is" and "Cum On Everybody."

As he later told *Sleazenation*, he'd first experienced thoughts of taking his own life after his Uncle Ronnie's death. "Right before I got my record deal, I was like, 'I'm twenty-three years old, I'm not going to get a record deal, shit is not going to work out for me.' I was in the studio one night and swallowed a bunch of pills. I was like, 'Yo, I gotta go to the hospital' but I threw this shit up out of my stomach before I had to get my stomach pumped. I threw up all over my man's basement studio. I was trying to do vocals to a song that's on my album now."

The song he was working on at the time, appropriately enough, was "Rock Bottom."

"I'll tell you why I took a bunch of pills on purpose," he continued. "There was a record label that was stringing us along for six months, telling us they wanted to sign me . . . I found out that that dude worked in the mailroom of the label. That same night I thought, fuck it, I don't wanna live no more. It was depressed-type shit.

"I took a bunch of pain killers, Tylenol. I took thirteen, sixteen of 'em and fuckin' threw 'em up. I thought I was going to die, I thought I was going to die for real . . . When that shit happened my body was numb. I wasn't even thinking. I had my fuckin' face in the toilet saying, 'I'm goin' to die! I'm probably goin' to die! Fuck it.' But my body was numb from the Tylenol and didn't really feel it. My head was spinning, I remember the room looked like everything going in circles. I was really fucked up.

"I was scared to tell my girl what happened, I told her I just got sick and was drunk at the studio. My boys looked out for me; they tried to keep my head up the next day because I was still depressed. We was all depressed because FBT had a lot of money invested in me and they didn't know if they were going to make their money back, so they were depressed. But they was trying to keep my head up because they knew what I was going through. I had no job, I couldn't buy my daughter diapers. It was just a fucked-up time. The funny thing is, less than a month later Dre called us and shit was all good, you know what I'm saying?"

While *The Slim Shady EP* helped to establish Eminem as one of hip-hop's most explosive new artists, he also maintained his rising street cred with guest appearances on other artists' records. He and his Detroit compadre Royce the 5'9" collaborated on the *Bad Meets Evil* EP, which featured two tracks, "Nuttin' to Do" and "Scary Movies"; Em and Royce would later reteam on the *Slim Shady LP* track that bore the same name as the EP.

Eminem also put in an appearance on underground MC Shabaam Sahdeeq's Rawkus Records' 12-inch "Five Star Generals," an underground hit that helped to raise Em's profile outside of his hometown—and in Japan, where the disc was a cult hit.

He was also inducted as a member of the Outsidaz, a respected extended-family New Jersey MC crew that had previously appeared on The Fugees' multiplatinum album *The Score*.

Em's rising visibility and mounting word-of-mouth helped to win him a slot on MTV's first *Lyricist Lounge* tour (he'd previously appeared on the show of the same name), which gave him the opportunity to perform before a national audience.

Eminem officially signed with Aftermath Records in January 1998. His friend and fellow D-12 member, Bizarre, recalls, "He was missing for three weeks. Nowhere to be found. Then he just up and called out of the blue: 'Yo, man, I just signed with Doctor Dre! He's got this fresh condo out here; you got to see it!' "

Artist and producer headed into the studio almost immediately to begin working on new material for the state-of-the-art album that would mark Em's major-label debut. During the adrenaline-fueled sessions that followed, the two new collaborators developed a powerful creative rapport, which yielded three of *The Slim Shady LP*'s most esteemed tracks, "My Name Is," "Role Model" and "Guilty Conscience"—the latter an Eminem/Dr. Dre duet.

"It was a dream come true for me," Em says. "I had to shake the butterflies at first. But it was also anxiousness to just get in there and show him what I could do. Ever since the first day we got in the studio and got down, I knew we had a chemistry."

The pair began their studio adventure with some loose freestyle experiments, two of which eventually grew into full-blown album tracks. "As soon as we went into the studio we knocked out four songs in six hours," Em says, adding, "Every beat he would make, I had a rhyme for." Indeed, the partnership clicked so strongly that Dre subsequently invited Eminem to contribute to his own *2001* album.

Months before its February 23, 1999, release, Eminem's Aftermath/Interscope debut, *The Slim Shady LP* had already generated an unprecedented level of pre-release buzz and word-of-mouth excitement, both in the hip-hop underground and the mainstream music business.

Em stirred up interest with a national tour several months before the album's release, while Aftermath/Interscope fanned the flames with a pre-album single, "Just Don't Give a Fuck," backed with "Brain Damage." That release became a Top Ten rap single in the early weeks of 1999, and did an effective job of setting the stage for the album's long-form verbal assault.

"Just Don't Give a Fuck" (to which fellow rising Detroit white boy Kid Rock contributed some cut-up work) was a bracing statement of purpose, with Eminem unleashing a stinging stream of lyrical invective, bragging of his excessive drug use and his dangerous driving habits, and making a vague reference to having an unnameable disease.

That auspicious introduction was followed by an even more memorable calling card, the cosmically unhinged anthem "My Name Is," produced and co-written by Dr. Dre. An appropriately all-over-the-place evocation of Slim Shady's goofy/malevolent dichotomy, with an insidiously infectious hook to match, "My Name Is" finds Em facetiously inviting kids to follow his example while simultaneously demonstrating why doing so would be a bad move.

"My Name Is" was a cinch to generate controversy, what with Slim expressing his desire to impregnate a Spice Girl and claiming that he "ripped Pamela Lee's tits off" and stapled his junior high school English teacher's "nuts to a stack of paper." He also reveals that his "mom does more dope than I do" and that he dreams of slitting his absentee father's throat.

But much of the general public became acquainted with "My Name Is" through the extensive airplay of its promotional video, an appropriately loony concoction which found Slim Shady spoofing a parade of familiar faces ranging from President Clinton to Eminem's Interscope labelmate Marilyn Manson. The clip also presented a relatively family-friendly variation on Em's outlaw persona, with a considerably toned-down variation of the song's original lyrics. The deceptively non-threatening video gave middle America its first concentrated dose—if a somewhat watered-down one—of Eminem's goofy anticharisma, and this relatively cuddly variation on his volatile persona was almost immediately embraced by unsuspecting kids across the country.

The pre-album buzz was reflected in the extensive media coverage that Em received in the months before *The Slim Shady LP*'s release, with prominent pieces in such publications as *Rap Pages*, *The Source*, *Spin*, *Stress*, *URB* and *Vibe*.

Spin, for instance, rhapsodized, "Imaginatively unhinged and bearing a thesaurus full of insults, Eminem comes off like a white-trash Don Rickles who grew up worshipping LL Cool J."

The *Los Angeles Times* even took the unusual step of doing a major feature on February 7, two weeks before the album's release date. Even then, some soon-to-be-familiar critical themes were prominent in the paper's coverage, anticipating the controversy that would follow him for the rest of the year.

By this point, the rap community and the wider music industry was abuzz with excitement over Eminem. The advance buzz on the album was so strong that Interscope took the unprecedented step of manufacturing an initial shipment of one million copies.

6

Unlike most relatively unknown new rap artists—particularly white ones—Eminem arrived on mass-media radar with established credentials. The combination of the skills he'd demonstrated on his indie EP and the credibility-building participation of Dr. Dre allowed him an aura of legitimacy that dispelled any notions of a Vanilla Ice–style hype long before his album hit the streets.

The Slim Shady LP fully lived up to the advance hype, making it clear that there was abundant talent and vision—albeit a decidedly idiosyncratic talent and a supremely twisted vision—behind Eminem's taboo-shattering tales, whose liberal doses of profanity and offhanded references to murder, date rape, drug use and all manner of macabre misbehavior were quite unlike anything previously heard in the rap idiom.

While verbal outrage and violent imagery were certainly nothing new in the extreme-prone world of hardcore hip-hop, the verbal craft and cinematic detail of Eminem's rhymes were in a class of their own. Melding twisted humor, outlandish fantasy and hallucinatory violence, Em created a cohesive and disturbing alternate reality which *The Source* likened to "a place where *Natural Born Killers* meets *Pee-Wee's Playhouse*."

The artist delivered his colorfully sadistic scenarios of aggression and revenge in a distinctively nasal—some might say whiny—voice that was prone to break into a gallery of cartoony alternate personalities at the drop of a hat.

The Slim Shady LP features its fair share of straight-up gangsta-style bragging, but even that receives an outlandishly original spin. Eminem's ever-present consciousness of his own insecurities and his acute awareness of the general absurdity of existence give his boasts an element of slapstick self-doubt that guarantees that they never proceed along conventional lines.

The album—on which the FBT Productions team handled production duties for all but the three tracks that Dr. Dre produced—commences with a "Public Service Announcement," a pointedly tongue-in-cheek verbal parental-advisory sticker on which co-producer Jeff Bass, in his most mellifluous tones, states, "The views and events expressed here are totally fucked, and are not necessarily the views of anyone. However, the events and suggestions that appear on this album are not to be taken lightly . . . Slim Shady is not responsible for your actions." At the end of the announcement, Slim himself advises, somewhat facetiously, "Don't do drugs."

That opening salvo sets the stage for the anthemic "My Name Is," which is followed by the Eminem/Dr. Dre epic "Guilty Conscience," which puts a sardonic modern spin on the old angel/devil cartoon dilemma, as Em and Dre engage in a heated moral debate on a trio of potentially violent scenarios. In the first, Dre advises a would-be liquor store thief to consider the consequences of his action, while Em suggests that he go ahead with the robbery, kill the store's elderly female clerk and then elude the cops by dressing in drag. In the second vignette, Em encourages the protagonist to drug and rape the fifteen-year-old girl he's picked up at a rave party, while Dre urges him to do the right thing and keep his hands off.

In the concluding segment of "Guilty Conscience," the main character comes home to find his wife in bed with another man. Eminem insists that the husband cut the woman's head off; Dre suggests that he stop and think about the couple's baby before he does something he'll regret. Em cheekily points to Dre's own violent past, taunting his mentor by referring to a much-publicized physical confrontation with MTV personality Dee Barnes. Dre responds that he's learned from his mistakes, and that the cuckolded character "don't need to go the same route that I went," before abruptly coming over to

Em's side and advising the poor guy to shoot his wife and her lover.

On "Brain Damage," Em recalls his suffering at the hands of bullies when he was a teenager. After flamboyantly faking an appendicitis attack in class in an attempt to avoid an after-school fight with a bully, he's assaulted in the boys' room by the aforementioned D'Angelo Bailey, before Em retaliates with a carefully applied broomstick to his tormentor's skull. But upon returning home, Em blacks out due to the brain damage he'd sustained from prior beatings, to the extent that his brain falls out of his skull and has to be sewn back in.

On "Role Model," Eminem launches a preemptory strike on the aura of controversy that would soon surround him. In the process, he fantasizes tearing out Vanilla Ice's dreadlocks, slapping Garth Brooks and giving First Lady Hillary Rodham Clinton grief over her husband's sexual peccadilloes after she accuses him of being a pervert.

Elsewhere on "Role Model," Shady confesses to having murdered Nicole Brown Simpson and Ron Goldman, while admitting that he's "been with ten women who got HIV" and is "dumb enough to ask for a date with Lauryn Hill." He also hangs himself from a tree with his own penis, and envisions his own drug-overdose death and subsequent return from the grave. And when he states, "Mother, I love you/I never meant to hit you over the head with that shovel," it's not quite clear whether he's quoting Norman Bates or fantasizing about his own mom.

"My Fault"—with Eminem revealing his singing chops on the Latin-tinged chorus—finds Slim taking an uncharacteristically remorseful stance, after meeting ex-heroin addict Susan at a rave, and inadvertently allowing her to overdose on psychedelic mushrooms. While Susan hallucinates that he is her sexually abusive father, a panicky Em attempts to call an ambulance and is eventually left sobbing when she dies.

The up-tempo "Cum On Everybody," which Em introduces as "my dance song," is a relatively carefree number in which the star admits that he's "one Excedrin tablet short of a full medicine cabinet" and announces that he's "freestylin' every verse that I spit/'cos I don't even remember the words to my shit," while guest vocalist Dina Rae coos seductively. He also confides that he "gave a girl herpes in exchange for syphilis" and that he has "full-blown AIDS and a sore throat." He also claims, "I tried suicide once and I'll try it again/That's why I write songs where I die at the end."

"As the World Turns" offers a parallel-universe soap opera in which Em recalls "slappin' teachers and jackin' off in front of my counselors" in school and getting so high on crack, coke and smack that he doesn't let the fact that his back is broken keep him from fucking a "fat slut" to death with his "go-go gadget dick." The track also features an on-target premonition of Em's soon-to-be success: "We drive around in million dollar sports cars/While little kids hide this tape from their parents like bad report cards."

Slim sings again on the funky, drug-obsessed chorus of "I'm Shady," whose melody was inspired by Curtis Mayfield's *Superfly* classic "Pusherman." In the song, Em says once again that he has AIDS, claims that his "teacher sucked my wee-

wee in pre-school" and further explores his suicide obsession, stating that he'd like to "blow my brain out/just to see what it feels like" and that he doesn't "want to just die a normal death/I wanna be killed twice." On the same number, Shady insists that he'll plagiarize material from other rappers' demo tapes and complains that he's broke, despite having had a Number One club hit, because "people don't buy shit no more/they just dub it." He also offers a lengthy list of the substances he does and doesn't ingest (yes to pills, beer and 'shrooms; no to crack, coke and heroin).

But *The Slim Shady LP*'s most controversial track was the harrowing " '97 Bonnie and Clyde," in which Eminem describes murdering his estranged girlfriend, mopping up the bloody scene with the help of the couple's young daughter and dumping the corpse in a lake. The track is made even all the more disturbing by the knowledge that it features Em's own three-year-old daughter Hailie Jade, and that the narrative was inspired by his feelings toward the girl's mother, his on-again, off-again girlfriend Kim, with whom he'd maintained a volatile but oddly durable relationship for several years. The deceptively bucolic-sounding track starts off sounding like a loving tribute to Hailie, before abruptly turning homicidal.

Even at their most antisocial and unsavory, there was no denying the rich detail and head-spinning maliciousness of Eminem's rhymes, and his vocal delivery compensated in character and quirkiness whatever it lacked in technical precision.

"I've tried to take [my music] in another direction," he told the *Los Angeles Times*. "I've got to be different. Rap, overall, is entertainment. I'm trying to bring it in an entertaining way that's clever—you never know what's going to come, what I'm going to say next. I try to catch people off guard with punch lines. I catch myself off guard a lot of times when I'm writing it. If you're not different, you're gonna lose."

The Slim Shady LP's general vibe of disenfranchisement and resentment extended to the album's list of acknowledgments, which ended with the statements, "To the people I forgot, you weren't on my mind for some reason and you probably don't deserve any thanks anyway," and "To all the people who never gave love and continue to deny me 'cuz of what I look like: suck my dick you fucks!!!"

Following its release on February 23, 1999, *The Slim Shady LP* achieved the virtually unheard-of feat of entering the *Billboard* album charts at number two, selling a reported 480,000 copies in its first two weeks. By May, the album had been certified double platinum for domestic sales of two million copies. By the end of the year, *The Slim Shady LP* had sold over three million.

One early signal of the magnitude of Eminem's new stardom was his presence on the cover of *Rolling Stone*—a magazine not exactly known for championing rap artists—in late April.

The *Rolling Stone* piece also featured some memorable photos, including a grimacing, paint-covered Em, Em as a briefcase-toting preppie talking on a pay phone, and a naked Em showing off his tattoos ("Eminem" and "Slim Shady" on his right and left biceps, respectively, and "Kim" and "Rot in Pieces" on his abdomen) and holding an apparently lit stick of dynamite over his crotch.

In a three-star review of his album, *USA Today* observed, "Much has been made over Eminem's being white, but his real differences from other rappers are more than skin deep. Rather than rapping about the high life, he reflects on hitting 'Rock Bottom' or how he might get some payback if he ever had the cash. He admits to being 'one sandwich short of a picnic basket,' and after hearing him explain to his infant daughter why Mommy is 'sleeping' in the trunk of the car, who'd argue?"

Inevitably, *The Slim Shady LP*'s rampant sales success went hand-in-hand with the intense media furor over his raucous lyrics. Many critics—not to mention parents of the young kids who'd initially been won over by the toned-down "My Name Is" video—were horrified by the lyrics' cheerfully vicious mayhem.

While some recognized the album's cartoonish imagery as the hip-hop equivalent of the slapstick gore of director Sam Raimi's *Evil Dead* film series, others were considerably less amused. At a time of an increasing backlash against violent images in film, television and music, Eminem's sacrilegious lyrical content made a distinctly inviting target for attacks by morally outraged critics from all ends of the political and social spectrum. His inflammatory tales were condemned by women's groups, critics fervently debated the merits of his work, and *Billboard* editor Timothy White excoriated him for "making money by exploiting the world's misery."

"The world will get offended when they listen to my shit," Eminem acknowledged at one point, adding, "At the end of the day, I don't give a shit what I rapped about. I'm just having fun—and making fun of all the fucked-up shit in the world."

His detractors may dismiss him as a misogynistic homophobe who glorifies the human spirit's darkest attributes, but the emotional truths underlying Eminem's extravagantly nasty rhymes are considerably more complex and difficult to pin down. One might condemn his supposed advocacy of extreme misbehavior, but it's hard to deny the material's darker psychological resonance. Indeed, it's worth noting that Eminem is the only hip-hop artist in recent memory who actually *brags* about his low self-esteem, and the artful construction of his rhymes makes it hard to just write him off as an embittered crackpot.

Though he's been quoted as saying "I do promote violence and I don't give a fuck," Em disputes critics' claims that his work encourages socially deviant behavior. "I grew up listening to 2 Live Crew and N.W.A.," he says, "and I never went out and shot nobody."

He adds, "*Saving Private Ryan* was probably the illest, sickest movie I've ever watched, and I didn't see anybody criticizing that one for violence.

"A lot of my rhymes are just to get chuckles out of people. Anybody with half a brain is going to be able to tell when I'm joking and when I'm serious.

"My album isn't for younger kids to hear," this devoted dad told *Rolling Stone*. "It has an advisory sticker, and you must be eighteen to get it. That doesn't mean younger kids won't get it, but I'm not responsible for every kid out there. I'm not a role model, and I don't claim to be."

In his more analytical moments, Eminem has endeavored to put the controversy in perspective by pointing out the fantasy element in his writing, and reminding his critics that he's not actually advocating the activities portrayed in his out-there tales.

"My thoughts are so fucking evil when I'm writing shit," he admits, adding, "If I'm mad at my girl, I'm gonna sit down and write the most misogynistic fucking rhyme in the world. It's not how I feel in general, it's how I feel at the moment."

But he also maintains that he's honestly portraying the emotional circumstances that lie behind such unsavory behavior, and that he isn't likely to engage in such activities himself.

"I'm not alone in feeling the way I feel. I believe that a lot of people can relate to my shit—whether white, black, it doesn't matter. Everybody has been through some shit, whether it's drastic or not so drastic. Everybody gets to the point of 'I don't give a fuck.'

"I do say things that I think will shock people," he says. "But I don't *do* things to shock people. I'm not trying to be the next Tupac, but I don't know how long I'm going to be on this planet. So while I'm here, I might as well make the most of it."

Marshall Mathers III has been described by friends as a complicated, intense young man who's a hyperactive clown when he's in character, but a rather shy—and sometimes almost painfully sensitive—loner when he's out of the public eye. And while many of *The Slim Shady LP*'s outrageously violent images are presented as giddy manifestations of his most hateful impulses, on the more overtly serious numbers "If I Had" and "Rock Bottom," he temporarily drops the mask of goofball bravado to reveal the bruised feelings that remain from his harsh early history.

"If I Had" catches Eminem sounding genuinely frustrated and pissed off, angrily addressing the harshness of life and

© Vinnie Zuffante. Attending the 1999 Source Hip Hop Music Awards in L.A.

© Vinnie Zuffante. Attending the 1999 Source Hip Hop Music Awards in L.A.

© Vinnie Zuffante. Backstage at the 1999 MTV Video Music Awards in NYC.

© Vinnie Zuffante. Arriving at the 1999 MTV Video Music Awards in NYC.

© V.D.L. Attending the MTV European Music Awards in Ireland.

© Chuck Pulin. Backstage at the 1999 MTV Video Music Awards in NYC.

© Chuck Pulin. Backstage at the 1999 MTV Video Music Awards in NYC.

© Sian Kennedy. Eminem.

the frustrations of poverty. He also bemoans the state of his career, expressing biting resentment toward other less talented but more successful rappers.

"Rock Bottom" is even more affecting in its raw-nerved evocation of the cumulative frustrations of life on society's economic margins, with the artist sounding as if he might lose his grip at any moment. The overall effect is riveting, providing a sharp contrast to Eminem's prevailing image as sharp-tongued smart-ass.

In a review in New York's *Village Voice*, Barry Walters pinpointed much of Eminem's contradictory appeal, calling him "the most disturbing entertainer I've cared about in years . . . Eminem most definitely is a knucklehead, but instead of making me angry, he makes me chuckle, wonder, even empathize. Yeah, I think he sometimes goes too far for a snicker or a shock, but that's part of his appeal.

"When he says he hates himself fifty-seven different ways during the course of *The Slim Shady LP*, I believe him. This loser plays his trailer-trash persona for laughs, but also pathos, and his ability to switch back and forth in the course of a single rhyme is what some people—even I—find upsetting . . . In interviews, he says you should be able to tell when he's kidding. But you can't, and that ambiguity is exactly what has always given his dark comedy and horror heritage—from *Pink Flamingos* to *South Park*, *Frankenstein* to *Evil Dead 2*—its bite.

"Eminem admits he's a monster," Walters continues. "If we're to trust his lyrics, he takes the scariest drugs, terrorizes fat girls, staples his junior high school teacher's nuts to a stack of papers. He also alludes to suicide attempts, being bullied constantly as a kid, undergoing shock therapy. And he says he has a disease they can't name. It could—as he suggests several times throughout the album—be AIDS. Eminem admits he's scared to get tested, and given all his boasting about his sexual and drug history, he's got reason to be nervous."

In a separate *Village Voice* review, Walters' colleague Toure articulated certain reservations that African-American observers have expressed about Eminem's success, asking, "Does our dislike of him start with our ears or our politics, or cultural discomfort with whites walking on our turf? Or is it that he's just wack? Does the love for him in a large segment of the Black hip-hop community start with the ears or with a perverse pleasure in the expansion of hiphop—a joy that the national conversation that is hiphop may now begin to tackle the fucked-upness of white people?"

The level of controversy surrounding Eminem attests to the button-pushing potency of his work, all the more so because his audience includes so many young white pop fans who rarely listen to hip-hop otherwise.

"You can't control who likes you," Em says. "If I got Backstreet Boy fans what am I supposed to do? Turn them away? Whoever likes my stuff, likes my stuff. But just know Slim Shady is hip-hop. I grew up on hip-hop, it's the music I love and it's the music I respect. I respect the culture; that's me."

One obvious manifestation of Eminem's straddling of the hip-hop underground and mainstream pop stardom is the creation of airplay-friendly—and often substantially altered—"clean" versions of his work, reworked minus profanity for mass consumption. Rather than simply editing out or bleeping the offending lyrics, Em and his producers have taken a more creative path to airplay-friendliness.

For example, the PG-rated reworking of "My Fault" kept the song's chorus (which borrows its hook from the fifties' pop hit "I Will Follow Him") intact, but altered the original storyline so that Susan now dies from an allergic reaction to mushrooms—the non-hallucinogenic kind—on her pizza. Though the sanitized "Pizza version" was at one point planned for release as a single, it ended up debuting on the companion album to MTV's popular animated series *Celebrity Deathmatch*—hence the hyperactive claymation Eminem featured in the video.

Meanwhile, the "Guilty Conscience" video, which extended the song's original concept with a special-effects-heavy lyrical face-off between Em and Dr. Dre, cleaned up the original lyrics with toned-down new language, while replacing the original's stop-start vocal breaks with an added verse that made the song flow more smoothly.

The video, which features veteran actor

Robert Culp as onscreen narrator, was heavily edited by MTV prior to its premiere on the network on May 18, 1999. "I sent MTV a copy of the video," Em reported, and because they are on this antiviolence campaign because of the Columbine killings, they edited the fuck out of the video."

"When I was growin' up, I wanted to rap about shit people were scared to rap about," Eminem stated in an interview with *The Source*. "If I'm *thinkin'* about it, I'm gonna say it. I make a lot of my own personal business public. There are things I'm gonna say in my life that other people will think is embarrassing to them."

One of the many deeply personal areas of Eminem's nonmusical life that he's explored in his work is his on-again, off-again relationship with Kim Scott, the mother of his daughter Hailie Jade. The couple's long-standing but decidedly volatile romance has been the source of much curiosity amongst fans and media observers, and a consistent source of perverse inspiration for the artist.

The combination has reportedly always been a combustible one, and the couple has broken up and reunited several times. At one point in 1997, while they were split up, Kim, according to Marshall, made it difficult for him to see his daughter, going so far as to threaten him with a restraining order.

"Shit got worse when my daughter was born," Em says. "Every time we would fight and we'd break up, she'd say 'Well, if you don't want to see me anymore, you can't see Hailie.' She would use my daughter against me."

The turbulent relationship has often been portrayed, sometimes in a disturbingly harrowing manner, in Eminem's rhymes, most obviously—and gruesomely—on the *Slim Shady LP*'s " '97 Bonnie and Clyde," aka "Just the 2 of Us."

The *Slim Shady LP* version of the song is all the more disturbing for the fact that Hailie appears as herself on the track. She's also pictured on the album's front cover with her dad; both are standing on a dock, looking out at the water, while the bare feet of a presumably dead (and presumably female) body stick out of the open trunk of a car parked nearby.

Eminem related the circumstances of his daughter's guest appearance to *Rolling Stone*: "I lied to Kim and told her I was taking Hailie to Chuck E. Cheese that day. But I took her to the studio. When she found out I used our daughter to write a song about killing her, she fucking blew. We had just got back together for a couple of weeks. Then I played her the song, and she bugged the fuck out."

In an interview with the adult magazine *Black Gold*, he further explained. "What I told her was like, 'Look, I was pissed off!' That's all I could say. I really felt that I wanted to do that shit. At one point in time, I really wanted to do that shit. For-real baby-momma drama."

He's also stated that his daughter has heard " '97 Bonnie and Clyde," but is still too young to grasp the subject matter. He promises that he'll put things into perspective for her when she's old enough to understand. "I'll let her know that Mommy and Daddy weren't getting along at the time. None of it was to be taken literally."

It's Eminem's tenderhearted devotion to his daughter—which is obvious, and even poignant, even when he's talking about killing her mother—that lifts " '97 Bonnie and Clyde" above garden-variety gangsta brutality. Not only does Eminem dedicate *The Slim Shady LP* to her, but her name is tattooed on his right arm.

In the *Rolling Stone* story, Eminem's longtime pal Proof shed some light on Em and Kim's embattled relationship. "One time we came home and Kim had thrown all his clothes on the lawn—which was, like, two pairs of pants and some gym shoes. So we stayed at my grandmother's, and Em's like, 'I'm leaving her, I'm never going back.' Next day, he's back with her. The love they got is so genuine, it's ridiculous. He's gonna end up marrying her. But there's always gonna be conflict there."

Even after his album had hit the double-platinum mark, Em still resided with Hailie and Kim in a mobile home previously occupied by his mother, situated in a Detroit trailer park. "After I got my record deal, my mother moved back to Kansas City," he explained to *Rolling Stone*. "I took over the payments on her trailer."

Since his rise to fame, the artist has continued to work with longtime cohorts from his Detroit days, like Proof, Royce and DJ Head, who are all part of his live show, and longtime manager/lawyer Paul "Bunyan" Rosenberg, who even gets his own track on *The Slim Shady LP*, via a genuine-sounding answering-machine message asking his client to "tone [the album] down a little bit." "The same friends I had back then are the same people on tour with me now," Em says. "I don't want them to be poor."

Journalists who've interviewed Em often seem surprised with his relatively reserved, self-effacing manner, and charmed by the impish humor that emerges once he relaxes his guard. Many who've spent time with him paint a picture of a mischievous man-child who's prone to spontaneously break into freestyle rhyme or bizarre character voices, but also a sensitive soul whose confidence can still be bruised by a careless callous comment. By all accounts, he enjoys a rowdy good time, but also maintains a shy, private, introspective side that few outsiders can penetrate.

The fact that Eminem is Caucasian is inevitably a significant element of his identity. Having grown up as part of an economically disadvantaged dysfunctional family adds another level to the outsider status that's shaped his character and his music.

Em himself has always seemed reluctant to play the race card. "I try not to look at it that way, being white," he told the *Los Angeles Times*. "I don't wake up every day and look in the mirror, 'Oh, I'm white.' If it has helped me, the only way that it could have possibly helped me is by catching people off guard because they wouldn't expect it coming from a white MC."

But he acknowledges that his early experiences of rejection on the Detroit scene are still an influence on his work. "When you pop a *Slim Shady LP* in, you're gonna be able to tell what I went through. I don't really feel like it's hurt me, it's just affected me and I don't know if it's necessarily in a negative way. It's made me backlash at people, like, 'Fuck you.' I've taken a lot of crap in my life . . . I got to a point where I said I'm not taking it anymore."

Despite the fact that white acts like the Beastie Boys and 3rd Bass long ago demonstrated that race need not be a hindrance to making credible hip-hop, many in the national rap community have regarded Eminem's crossover success with varying degrees of suspicion. It's not hard to understand that reaction, given the presence of "My Name Is" on rock radio stations that would never touch a record by a black rap act.

"I'm white in a music started by black people. I'm not ignorant to the culture and I'm not trying to take anything away from the culture," he says in his defense. "But no one has a choice where they grew up or what color they are. If you're a rich kid or a ghetto kid, you have no control over your circumstance. The only control you have is to get out of your situation or stay in it.

"I do feel like I'm coming from a standpoint where people don't realize there are a lot of poor white people. Rap music kept my mind off all the bullshit I had to go through."

Understandably, Eminem seemed to grow progressively more annoyed as 1999 wore on, when the issue of race was brought up by journalists. "I get offended when people say, 'So, being a white rapper, and growing up white, after being born white . . .' It's all I ever hear!" he groused to *Vibe*.

"At this point, I'm like 'Come up with something new.' I hate the same old questions. But it seems like white magazines such as *Spin* and *Rolling Stone* focus on my whiteness more than black magazines. Like *The Source*. They're like, he's white, let's get over it. But when *Rolling Stone* came out with 'Low Down Dirty White

Boy' on the cover, I was like 'This shit is critical.' I liked the article inside, but when I saw the cover, I was like, 'What the fuck is this?!'

"But then you have your magazines like *XXL* that called me a culture stealer and an invader. That's some elementary school shit. Give me a break! It's funny how all the magazines can dwell on my race, but they could *never* say that my shit is wack because they know my shit is tight!

"All my life I've been dealing with my race because of where I grew up and being in the rap game. I'm at a boiling point . . . Anybody who pulls the race card is getting it right back in their face.

"Unless you want to fuck me," Em reasons, "why do you care what I look like?"

One sure sign of Eminem's rising popularity has been the existence of a series of recordings by other hip-hop artists impugning Slim's authenticity, his rhyming abilities and/or his originality.

One of these was fellow white rapper Milkbone, whom Eminem had name-checked on "Just Don't Give a Fuck" alongside MC Serch and Pete Nice of 3rd

Bass. Milkbone responded with an unflattering lyric on "Introducing Milkbone," a track on Death Row Records' various-artists compilation *The Chronic 2000*.

"I wasn't even dissing Milkbone on my album," Em states. "When I said 'I'm on a Serch to crush a Milkbone,' I was talking about stereotypes and now I heard he wants to bring it, so he could bring it and look stupid, you know what I'm sayin'? I heard his shit and his shit is garbage. I wish it was dope enough for me to respond, but it's not, you know what I'm sayin'?"

Meanwhile, Em found himself drawn into a feud with Cage, a New York rapper who has apparently claimed that Eminem copped his style. On "Role Model," Em refers to recording over a Cage cassette.

"I didn't know any of this shit was going to happen between Cage and me," Em claimed. "I dissed Cage because he said I took his style. I don't even know the motherfucker! Never even heard of him! My manager, as a matter of fact, had to send me a copy of his record. I heard his record and I was like, 'This motherfucker don't even sound like me!' "

One of Eminem's more colorful feuds, though, was an ongoing verbal tiff with clown-faced Detroit rap-metallists Insane Clown Posse. While appearing on the MTV phone-in advice show *Loveline*, Eminem responded to a viewer's question about the ICP situation: "First of all, they're already out of line, and there's not really much they can do to me, like as far as talent-wise, I feel. So there's not even a reason to respond to what they've been saying. I don't even know if it's a feud, I don't know what it is.

"To me personally, they're not rappers. They may be entertainers, but they're not entertainers when it comes to hip-hop music, and they're not hip-hop, they're not rap and they're not anything. So they're not in my field, so it's not really my place to say. They've dissed me on record . . . and it's not even worth me responding back to. I don't want to pay the studio time to even make a record to diss them."

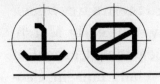

For Eminem, the dizzying year that followed *The Slim Shady LP*'s release—and his near-instant rise to stardom—was an intensive whirlwind of promotion, live performances and assorted public mayhem, interspersed with occasional work on the follow-up album that he would release in the spring of 2000.

Despite the aura of controversy that had begun surrounding him before his album had even hit the streets, the upstart MC quickly established himself as a multimedia personality, making memorable appearances on such appropriate outlets as MTV's *Total Request Live* and notorious shock-jock Howard Stern's freewheeling radio and TV shows. In early March, Em performed for a beachfront crowd of adoring (and scantily clad) fans in Cancun, Mexico, as part of MTV's *Spring Break '99* broadcast.

Eminem's controversial reputation didn't seem to be much of a hindrance on the weekend of March 13, when he was treated as a conquering hero with a series of homecoming honors in Detroit, including a meeting with mayor Dennis Archer, who presented him with the key to the city. An MTV video crew was in attendance for the festivities, which included some radio-station appearances and an impromptu performance/autograph session at Em's old retail haunt Record Time, which brought out a news crew from the local ABC TV affiliate.

"It's good to be home," Em said at the time, absorbing the ironic spectacle of his new status as a respectable, in-demand celebrity. "It's crazy. It's like something you want to happen, but you don't know if it's going to, and then when it happens you're like, 'Whoa!' "

On April 7, Eminem kicked off the official Slim Shady Tour in Chicago, the first stop on a twenty-city U.S. headlining trek, with the Beatnuts, Mixmaster Mike, Last Emperor and Pace Won of the Outsidaz as opening acts on various nights. Em's new stage show—which also featured his Detroit MC cronies Proof and Royce, as well as hometown turntablist DJ Head—boasted an imaginative visual presentation that reflected his quirky persona, complete with a backdrop featuring the mushroom-covered mobile home pictured in *The Slim Shady LP*'s cover insert, a live, dancing version of the mummy who's featured in the album art, and some oversized props—including a giant red prop telephone for the stage presentation of the audio verité comedic bit "Ken Kaniff."

The most unexpected element of Eminem's live show, though, may have been the racially mixed, rabidly moshing audiences whose fervor seemed more akin to the intensity of an arena rock crowd. Early on, the Slim Shady Tour attracted controversy, not for its lyrical content but because some observers inaccurately accused Eminem of lip-synching to pre-recorded tapes on stage.

On May 8, in the audience for the first of two sold-out Eminem shows at Los Angeles' House of Blues—which featured a guest appearance by Dr. Dre, who showed up to perform his hit "Ain't Nuthin' But a 'G' Thang" with Em—was film star Dustin Hoffman, who'd brought his kids along for the occasion. Visiting with Eminem backstage after the show, the actor—who, as the star of *Little Big Man* and *Tootise*, is no stranger to dressing up in public—asked if he could play the dancing mummy in the late show. Em obliged, and at the end of the late set, removed the mummy's bandages to unveil Hoffman's true identity, much to the crowd's delight.

The same month, Eminem ran into old acquaintance Kid Rock—another young, white, politically incorrect Detroiter, who like Em broke big in 1999 after several years honing his skills on the Motor City hip-hop scene—when he stumbled into Kid Rock's gold-record celebration at Duke's restaurant in New York.

"I guess great minds and people from Detroit think alike," Kid Rock told *Rolling*

Stone. "Eminem had just come in to get chicken nachos or something. What's the odds of him bumping into me in New York City? Last time I saw him was at Christmas at Best Buy in Detroit. We talked about doing some touring. A month later, I'm like, 'Well, I guess I'll be opening for him.' "

Kid Rock subsequently sang his pal's praises in an MTV interview. "I don't think he really blew up overnight," he said of Eminem. "I mean, his stuff did take off quick, no doubt about it. But that kid's been putting in work as long as I have, you know, as long as he's been down with hip-hop. And you can hear it in his rhymes and in his skills that he's not an overnight sensation, 'cause nobody can learn to rhyme like that overnight. That kid's a true MC and one of the best ones out there, no doubt about it."

Kid Rock paid a backstage visit on May 24, when Eminem was back in his hometown to perform a triumphant show at Detroit's State Theatre. Also in attendance was Dr. Dre, who performed his "Nuthin' But a 'G' Thang." "I flew him out here especially for you," Em told the audience, though he opted to premiere the new video for their "Guilty Conscience" duet on a video screen, rather than performing the tune live.

Reviewing the State Theatre show, *Detroit Free Press* music critic Brian McCollum observed, "If you were among the sparse crowds that dotted local hip-hop showcases where Eminem cut his teeth in recent years, Sunday night's gig was revelatory. The rapper looked and played the star in front of a sold-out crowd of three thousand and a marquee with his name on it, just a quick dash down I-94 from the east side neighborhood where he grew up."

Describing the scene, McCollum wrote, "His oversized white T-shirt drenched in sweat, and generously drinking bottled water, Eminem tramped the length of the stage, slapping hands with the front row and even daring—just briefly—to surf the crowd during 'As the World Turns.' The racially diverse crowd reacted most boisterously to the infectious stuff from Eminem's album, chanting along to most every verse."

The Detroit concert—during which the

star delivered some pointed verbal jabs at Insane Clown Posse and playfully mooned the crowd—also included an uncharacteristically sincere moment of tribute. Eminem and Proof paused before the show's encore to ask for a moment of silence in honor of D-12 associate Cornell Pitts, a twenty-two-year-old Detroit man who had been fatally shot the previous Friday during a fight on nearby Belle Isle.

In June, Eminem joined the prestigious Vans Warped Tour, as a last-minute replacement for rap-rock veterans Cypress Hill, who'd dropped out of the gig to concentrate on finishing their fifth album. The tour was scheduled to include thirty-one North American dates, beginning in San Antonio, Texas, on June 25 and ending in Miami, Florida, on July 31.

The tour was a big success, but it was not all smooth sailing. On July 18, fans in Hartford, Connecticut—in a club show that took place on a night off from the Warped tour—witnessed Eminem plummet six feet from the front of a wet, poorly lit stage. After a quick trip to a local hospital, where he was diagnosed with bruised ribs, he was well enough to travel to New York the following day for a guest spot on MTV's *Total Request Live*. His injuries forced him to sit out the Warped shows in Pittsburgh and Philadelphia, but he was back on his feet in time for the tour's visit to Buffalo, New York.

After wrapping up the Warped tour at the end of July, Slim spent a good chunk of August on a promotional trip to Europe, making stops in London, Stockholm, Amsterdam, Hamburg, Munich and Paris, before heading back to the States at the end of the month.

While in London, Em made a pants-dropping guest appearance at the club Scratch during a show by The High and Mighty. But it was Amsterdam, famous for its relaxed drug laws, that was apparently the promo tour's most inspirational stop. Reportedly, after sampling a goodly amount of the, uh, local color, Em went on a five-day writing binge that yielded five new compositions.

Eminem's first full-on tour of Europe followed in the fall, and was another smashing success. But the trek's scheduled launch on October 21 in Amsterdam had to be delayed a few days to accommodate a guest appearance with Dr. Dre on *Saturday Night Live* on October 23, during which the pair delivered "Forgot About Dre" from Dre's *2001* album, which had hit stores the week before.

The European tour finally began on October 25 in Oslo, Norway, followed by consecutive one-nighters in Stockholm, Berlin, Chemnitz, Vienna, Munich, Stuttgart, Zurich, Offenbach and Cologne, followed by a British swing that included a show in Manchester, two in London and one in Glasgow, before returning to the Continent for gigs in Amsterdam in November.

Eminem named the audience in Glasgow, Scotland, as the best crowd of the tour, while designating Chemnitz, Germany, as the location of the tour's worst food, and Stockholm, Sweden, as having the most attractive women. The tour's best after-show party was judged to be a Polydor UK-sponsored event at London's Astoria, at which Slim reportedly had his first encounter with absinthe, a fabled alcoholic beverage which is reputed to have hallucinogenic properties.

Despite its strong start, the European

tour had to be cut short in mid-November after Eminem came down with a chest infection that caused his doctor to recommend a week of bed rest, forcing the cancellation of the tour's final three shows in Copenhagen, Malmö and Hamburg.

A few days after returning home, Eminem was in Los Angeles to shoot a video for "Forgot About Dre"—a duet with Dr. Dre from Dre's long-awaited *2001* album—with noted director Phillip Atwell on the Universal Studios backlot.

On November 26, Eminem was back in Detroit for a one-off hometown gig, sharing the bill with his old crew, the Dirty Dozen and Royce the 5'9". That show also served as the public launch of Shady Records, the new label that Em and Paul Rosenberg had launched two months earlier in association with Aftermath/Interscope, with D-12 as its first signing.

Em announced that he planned to perform on, and act as executive producer of, D-12's first album for the label. "I'm going to be in there. I'm going to be on the album, and I'm gonna be there in the studio, creating stuff or whatnot. It's going to be dope, it's going to be hot. I'm bringing heat with this group."

Eminem's notoriety helped give a career boost to several of his longtime cronies. For instance, his frequent sidekick and fellow D-12 member Proof was the winner of *The Source* magazine's 1999 Unsigned Hype contest, while D-12 member Bizarre received a fair amount of attention for his 1999 *Attack of the Weirdos* EP, on which Em guested. Em's "bad" half, Royce the 5'9", scored a solo deal with Tommy Boy Records, for whom he began recording a solo debut album that would feature some collaborations with Eminem.

November also saw the limited release of a special enhanced edition of *The Slim Shady LP*, including the extra tracks "Get You Mad," "Hazardous Youth (A Cappella Version-Freestyle-1)" and "Greg (A Cappella Version-Freestyle-2)," along with a digital video program including the videos for "My Name Is," "Just Don't Give a Fuck," "Role Model" and "Guilty Conscience," along with performance and studio footage and an Eminem computer screensaver.

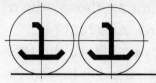

Despite his hectic workload of touring and promotion—not to mention his ongoing work on his follow-up to *The Slim Shady LP*— throughout 1999, Eminem managed to find time to make guest appearances on several other artists' records.

The most prominent of these was Slim's co-starring role in "Forgot About Dre," from Dr. Dre's *2001* album, the long-awaited sequel to his landmark solo debut *The Chronic*. The track—which also features a gurgly cameo by Hailie Jade—finds Dre and his motor-mouthed protégé delivering a rapid-fire verbal barrage announcing Dre's return to action in no uncertain terms, and taunting those who'd been foolish enough to count him out.

Elsewhere on *2001*, on "What's the Difference," Eminem proclaims his loyalty to Dre, offering his services if his label boss needs any of his enemies offed.

Em also contributed a raucous verse to the metallic "Fuck Off" on Kid Rock's breakthrough album *Devil Without a Cause*, and lent his voice to "Busa Rhyme" on Missy "Misdemeanor" Elliot's *Da Real World* album, as well as shooting his mouth off on such projects as OlWorlDisorder's "ThreeSixtyFive" single, The Madd Rapper's *Tell Em Why U Madd* album, Tony Touch's *Piecemaker* mixtape album, DJ Spinna's *Heavy Beats Volume One* and Rawkus Records' *Soundbombing 2* collection.

Em also added some verses to the remix of "Dead Wrong," from the Notorious B.I.G.'s posthumous *Born Again* album, while he and Dr. Dre contributed a track, "If I Get Locked Up Tonite," to Funkmaster Flex and Big Kap's *Tunnel* collection. He also did some recording with The Outsidaz, as well as playing the role of "The Mayor" in the video for Outsidaz main man Pace Won's underground hit "I Declare War."

Em also added tracks of his own to several various-artists albums. He contributed the typically loony *Slim Shady LP* outtake "Get You Mad" to DJs Sway and Tech's star-studded Interscope collection *This Or That*, as well as appearing on Sway and Tech's star-studded "The Anthem," a sonically spare posse cut whose who's-who guest list included RZA, Pharoahe Monch, Kool G Rap, Chino XL and KRS-ONE sharing the mic.

Em and Dr. Dre collaborated on the sonic shoot-'em-up "The Showdown," aka "Bad Guys Always Die," their contribution to the soundtrack album of the Will Smith/ Kevin Kline big-screen misfire *Wild Wild West*. The album also included tracks by former Fresh Prince Smith, Blackstreet, Guy, Faith Evans, Tatyana Ali and Enrique Iglesias, but most seemed to agree that "The Showdown"—a dark spaghetti-western epic with train whistles, wind effects, gunshots and operatic vocals—was both a standout on the album and one of Dre's most impressive productions to date.

The cleaned-up "Pizza Mix" version of "My Fault" showed up on Interscope's soundtrack companion album to MTV's *Celebrity Deathmatch*, alongside rap and rock tracks by Marilyn Manson, Xzibit, Last Emperor, Kool Keith, Primus, Lit and Stone Temple Pilots frontman Scott Weiland. It seems logical that the show's claymation spectacle of famous media stars beating the crap out of each other would hold some appeal for Eminem.

In late 1999, the previously unreleased Eminem track "Bad Influence" was featured on the soundtrack of the Arnold Schwarzenegger apocalypse-action flop *End of Days*, while a remixed version of his *Infinite*-era track "Murder Murder" showed up on the soundtrack disc for the popular hip-hop comedy *Next Friday*, which starred Dr. Dre's former N.W.A. bandmate Ice Cube.

At some point, Eminem also did some recording with another Interscope act, platinum retro-punks Limp Bizkit, though the fruits of that linkup had yet to see the light of day by the beginning of 2000.

Another collaboration that hasn't reached the ears of the public was an abortive teaming with another Interscope superstar, shock-rock icon Marilyn Manson. Though Em has stated that he passed on the opportunity to record with Manson because he feared that fans would consider it to be a blatant commercial move, rumors persist that the pair had planned to work on a " '97 Bonnie and Clyde" sequel together, until Manson saw the "My Name Is" video and took offense at the vignette spoofing him. Eminem reportedly went ahead and finished the song, now known as "Bitch So Wrong," without Manson's involvement.

Despite his numerous guest appearances on other artists' records, Eminem himself resists the persistent trend of having rampant star cameos all over his own work. Apart from the appearances of Dr. Dre and Royce the 5'9", and Kid Rock's low-key participation, *The Slim Shady LP* is refreshingly free of big-name guests.

"I wanted to show that I don't need

them other MCs," Em explained. "I can stand on my own. I can write my own [stuff] and make my own stuff dope. I've already got enough backing and enough credibility to where I don't need to ride anybody's coattails into the game.

"The trend right now in hip-hop is to get every dope rapper you can and get 'em on your album. But I'm not really a collaboration-type MC unless it's somebody that I'm extremely cool with. If I see somebody I like and respect, then I'm gonna get down with them. It has nothing to do with what type of music it is.

"A lot of the people who disrespected me are coming out of the woodwork now for collaborations. But I like doing my own shit. If there were too many other voices, the stories wouldn't go right."

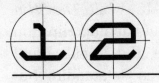

By the end of 1999, Eminem had racked up an impressive number of awards and nominations—as well as making some much-talked-about appearances on televised awards shows—to go along with *The Slim Shady LP*'s triple-platinum certification.

His first major awards victory—and perhaps one of the most personally fulfilling—occurred at the annual Detroit Music Awards, held April 23, 1999, at the Motor City's State Theatre, which saw Slim and Kid Rock cleaning up with several prizes each. Em prevailed in the categories of Outstanding Hip-Hop Act and Outstanding Hip-Hop MC, while *The Slim Shady EP* won for Outstanding Hip-Hop Recording. Meanwhile, Kid Rock's *Devil Without a Cause* won as Outstanding National Rock Album and his "I Am the Bullgod" took Outstanding National Rock Single, while the Kid was also named Outstanding Hip-Hop Producer.

For *The Source*'s Hip-Hop Music Awards, held at Los Angeles' Pantages Theatre on August 18 and televised on the UPN network two nights later, Eminem was up for Best New Artist, alongside Big Pun, Lauryn Hill, Juvenile and Noreaga. Em attended the awards show clad in a white T-shirt bearing the words "Kinky" and "Be All You Can Be," and broke into four-letter-word-strewn freestyles while being interviewed by reporters at the event. At one point, he was seen breaking away from the cameras to catch up with Limp Bizkit frontman Fred Durst.

On September 9, Eminem won three MTV Video Music Awards. The MTV awards show included a number of memorable highlights, including a fierce Em/

Dre performance of "Guilty Conscience." Upon winning Best New Artist, Eminem momentarily stepped out of Slim Shady mode to deliver a thoroughly endearing acceptance speech singling out his daughter for special thanks. Still, the outlaw had a hard time competing for attention with Lil' Kim, whose exposed left breast, covered only by a nipple-camouflaging pasty, was the talk of the evening. Following the awards show, Funkmaster Flex and Franchise Marketing threw a party honoring Em at El Flamingo in NYC.

On October 7, Eminem performed, alongside The Offspring, No Doubt, Cypress Hill and Chris Isaak, at ArtistDirect's first annual Online Music Awards—"designed to recognize excellence in music on the World Wide Web as determined by fans"—at Los Angeles' House of Blues. Those honors included several Internet-related awards. At the following month's Billboard Music Video Awards show, Em, Dre and director Philip Atwell all took home prizes when "Guilty Conscience" was cited as Best Rap/Hip-Hop New Artist Clip of the Year. On January 17, 2000, Em and Dre performed that tune again at the 1999 American Music Awards at Los Angeles' Shrine Theater.

The Slim Shady LP made a solid showing in numerous music critics' 1999 year-end surveys and best-of lists. *Rolling Stone*'s critics named him the year's Best, New Artist, while *USA Today* cited his album as one of the year's Top Ten albums, noting, "The first release on Dr. Dre's Aftermath label is a marvel of entertaining contradictions. The white rapper kicks himself mercilessly on one track, lashes out against the cruel world in the next, then vacillates between rage and apathy in razor-sharp tunes that visit a host of suburban miseries and comedies. He's unquestionably offensive, but the antidote for that venom can be found in the music's stinging humor and tight grooves."

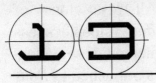

Throughout Eminem's first year at the top, the young star's personal life often seemed every bit as colorful, turbulent and downright bizarre as the tales he tells on record.

For one thing, he was sued by his own mother, Debbie Mathers-Briggs, for defamation, over his characterizations of her in interviews as an irresponsible, welfare-dependent drug user—and one with a habit of filing frivolous nuisance lawsuits.

The lawsuit, filed on September 10 in Macomb County Circuit Court in Mount Clemens, Michigan, sought ten million dollars in damages, claiming that Mathers-

Briggs had suffered damage to her reputation, emotional distress, loss of self-esteem, humiliation, sleeplessness and anxiety over statements her son allegedly made in interviews published in *Rolling Stone*, *Rap Pages* and *The Source* and broadcast on radio's *Howard Stern Show*.

The suit further claimed that Eminem had promised to help his mother with the mortgage on her mobile home but abruptly stopped making payments, causing the court to evict her from her home in late summer.

The publications named in the suit weren't the only ones in which Em had spoken about his mom in less-than-glowing terms. In the April issue of the online magazine *Addicted To Noise*, for instance, he recalled his rootless early days moving back and forth between Kansas City and Michigan, "My mother's a bitch. My mother never had a job. My mother never had nothing. We didn't have shit. We had to keep moving out of the house. I believe six months was the longest we ever lived in a house."

Eminem's defense against his mother's charges was straightforward. He simply maintained that he'd been telling the truth. As Paul Rosenberg stated shortly after the suit was filed, "Eminem's life is reflected in his music. Everything he said can be verified as true. Truth is an absolute defense to a claim of defamation."

Rosenberg further stated that the suit came as no surprise to his client. "His mother has been threatening to sue him since the success of his single 'My Name Is.' It is merely the result of a lifelong strained relationship between him and his mother. Regardless, it is still painful to be sued by your mother, and therefore the lawsuit will only be responded to through legal channels."

Still, Eminem admitted, "It's kind of a shitty feeling, like, damn, your mother's suing you. It doesn't bother me. I expected it."

Meanwhile, Debbie Mathers-Briggs' attorney, Fred Gibson, was quoted by the Associated Press as suggesting that Eminem's alleged distortion of his childhood was an attempt to overcompensate for being a white rapper in a predominantly black genre.

"He's a hip-hop artist," Gibson said. "Vanilla Ice went away a few years ago when his hard past was a fabrication. This isn't the same, but hip-hop is within the urban culture, and he's Caucasian, so he doesn't fit in. So he has to project this image."

On November 15, Rosenberg filed a motion to dismiss Mathers-Briggs' lawsuit, claiming that it lacked specific details of which of her son's statements she claimed to be untrue.

Soon after, Eminem squared off with another formidable opponent, the National Football League. The NFL had produced a series of popular promotional spots that used "My Name Is," renamed "My Name Is Joe" in tribute to Hall-of-Famers Joe Namath, Joe Gibbs, Joe Montana and "Mean" Joe Greene. But the campaign was quickly pulled off the air, possibly after someone actually got around to listening to the original version of the song.

Like many observers, Em was less surprised by the NFL dropping his song than by the fact that they had chosen to go anywhere near it in the first place. "I didn't know they were using it," he told the online magazine *Wall of Sound*, claiming that he saw the spots only once. "I was like, 'What the fuck?'

"It just makes me laugh, you know what I'm saying? I was laughing on the phone with my manager, like good, fuck 'em. It doesn't make any difference to me at all.

"People are so fucking stupid, man, to actually take my shit that seriously. I don't walk around and try to portray this gangster image, but the media has made me out to be that way, like I think I'm some kind of fuckin' white thug."

By the end of 1999, he'd found himself embroiled in yet another family feud, tangling this time with his maternal grandmother Betty Kresin, who objected to his plans to sample a section of a rap tape that he'd made in the mid-eighties with his late, beloved uncle Ronnie Polkinghorn.

Em had come across the homemade cassette and asked his grandmother—Ronnie's mother—for permission to use a forty-five-second snippet on his forthcoming album. Though she apparently agreed initially, she reportedly changed her mind after a dispute over a separate matter, threatening to sue if Em used the sample.

Kresin further excoriated her grandson

in print. "He's changed for the worse. He talks filthy to me and is angry and disrespectful," she told the *Detroit News*. "I don't know what's gotten into him.

"It gives me the creeps to think about it," Kresin said of Eminem's planned use of her son's voice. "I will not let my grandson destroy my dead son with this garbage. He's a bitter boy with sad songs who wants to make fame. Ronnie was a godly person."

Ironically, Kresin had recently spoken up in favor of Eminem when his mother filed her libel suit, telling the *Detroit News*, "That boy has always had it rough. I admire him for thriving and surviving despite it all."

Though Eminem insisted that he wanted to use the tape as a tribute to his uncle, he ultimately acceded to his grandmother's wishes and regretfully announced that he wouldn't be using the sample after all.

"My grandmother is going off on me," he told the *Detroit News*. "Now I don't think anything is going to happen. We grew up like brothers. I loved Ronnie. I've got a Ronnie tattoo on my arm. I wanted to pay tribute to him.

"I let the public decide for themselves what idiots my family is," he continued. "My family has never been there for me. They expect things because we're blood."

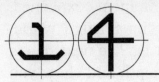

In November 1999, Eminem returned to the studio to finish recording his next album, which he announced would be titled *The Marshall Mathers LP*.

Dr. Dre, who produced five of the album's tracks, mixed four others and served as executive producer, said of their working methods, "We get in there, get bugged out, stay in the studio for fuckin' two days. Then you're dead for three days. Then you wake up, pop the tape in, like, 'Let me see what I've done.'"

The album's pointed monicker offered a clue to the new disc's more extreme, and more explicitly personal, lyrical content. "The last album," Eminem explained, "opened you up to Slim Shady's world, and how fucked up it is. The next one is going to go more in depth and show you why I got this way."

An announcement on the artist's Web site further described *The Marshall Mathers LP*'s thematic focus. "The next level is the side of Eminem that's possibly more frightening than Slim Shady. The side more disturbed than Eminem himself. The side that's been waiting in the shadows to spit rhymes at an unsuspecting public for years."

"It's angrier, I'll tell you that much," agreed Jeff Bass, one-half of the FBT production team. "This album, he's going out and saying what he really wants to say," he observed. "I read something that he wrote a long time ago about how he was going to get angrier and be more truthful about things on the second album, and he does exactly that."

Meanwhile, Eminem looked beyond the album to a variety of other creative avenues. His new label, Shady Records, along with manager Paul Rosenberg's company,

Goliath Artists, officially opened its doors in New York City in January 2000, with plans to release the first D-12 album later in the year.

Em has also spoken of a desire to pursue an acting career, and he shot four scenes, playing himself, for writer-director Dale Restighini's indie direct-to-video horror spoof, *Da Hip-Hop Witch*, which also featured the likes of Pras, Rah Digga and Killah Priest. According to *Entertainment Weekly*, though, Eminem suddenly got cold feet a few months before the film's scheduled August 2000 release, and asked to be cut out of the film.

On another occasion Em claimed, "I'm doing a feature film on my life. Me and Dre. Some of it's going to be true, and the other is gonna be some bugged-out shit. The other shit is how Dre views my life . . . It's gonna be bugged out!"

Beyond that project is his stated interest in a career in pornography. In an interview with the adult magazine *Black Gold*, Em expressed a desire to extend the revenge fantasies portrayed on *The Slim Shady LP* into a starring role in *A Day in the Life of Slim Shady*. "The concept," he explained, "would be me fucking all the girls that dissed me."

On New Year's Eve 1999, Eminem welcomed the new millennium at the fabled New York club, the Tunnel. The set included "If I Get Locked Up" (his and Dr. Dre's recent contribution to the Funkmaster Flex and Big Kap album that shares the club's name), "Forgot About Dre" and his verses from Notorious B.I.G.'s "Dead Wrong." After the show, Eminem and his posse moved on to the Manhattan nightspot, Chaos, where they spent the rest of the night at Puff Daddy's New Year's party.

Less than two months later, Eminem capped this phase of his career with the most prestigious of all of his 1999 awards, and the most indicative of how far he'd penetrated the mainstream pop-culture consciousness. He won Grammy awards for Best Rap Album and Outstanding Rap Solo Performance for "My Name Is"; he'd also been nominated, but didn't win, in the category of Best Duo or Group Performance for "Guilty Conscience."

As unpredictable as ever, Em failed to put in an appearance at the glitzy, televised awards show. He was elsewhere in

L.A., working with Dr. Dre on material for the still-in-progress *Marshall Mathers LP*.

"He didn't believe he'd win anything, and they were only televising one of the rap awards," Paul Rosenberg insisted to the online music-news site *Wall of Sound*. "So he thought his time would be better spent [in the studio]." Rosenberg further stated that Em was happy about winning, but added that "these things don't affect him like normal people."

FBT producers Jeff and Marky Bass were present at the Grammy show, but their client's absence meant that they didn't get to accept their Best Rap Album prizes on stage. "Because Eminem didn't show up, the whole thing changed," said Jeff. "If he would've showed up, they were going to have that Album of the Year award televised. But they didn't."

Eminem's Grammy no-show made it clear that the artist wasn't ready to go Hollywood. "You've got to keep that foundation because no matter how much you blow up, you gotta see those same people on the way down," Eminem states. "If you don't have a foundation to stand on, the platform's gonna fall out from under you."

Having spent most of his life living with rejection and disappointment, the still-rising star retained a healthy skepticism toward his own success, and often seems haunted by nagging doubts over whether he's worthy of such attention. "I couldn't even *get into* a motherfucking club just being Eminem, before the ['My Name Is'] video," he notes. "Last night they had people clearing tables for me. It's fucking bananas. Scary shit, too, 'cause you can fall just as quick as you went to the top."

In the months leading up to *The Marshall Mathers LP*'s release, the air of curiosity and anticipation surrounding the album mounted. Meanwhile, a bootleg Eminem CD entitled *Fucking Yzarc*—collecting various guest appearances and non-album tracks—circulated widely through underground channels. And the *Marshall Mathers LP* track "Kim," a prequel of sorts to " '97 Bonnie and Clyde," leaked out to fans months before the new album's release date, causing the artist to put his foot down and restrict the flow of music from the in-the-works project.

"Some motherfuckers already down-loaded that shit on the Internet," Eminem told *Sonicnet* early in 2000. "I've been keeping my album pretty locked down as far as songs. Once I saw that shit on the Internet, I just said, 'No more tapes, no more CDs are going out, or anything.'"

The Marshall Mathers LP's first single, "The Real Slim Shady"—a head-spinningly fluid declaration of war on Eminem's various adversaries—was originally sched-uled to be released to radio on April 21. But the track was leaked and traded online in the MP3 format, via such controversial music-trading software programs as Nap-ster and Gnutella, prompting Interscope to release it one week early.

By the time the album was released on May 23, 2000, Eminem had—either through canny media manipulation or his natural tendency to push people's buttons— already generated considerable public con-troversy. His reference on "The Real Slim Shady" to teen-pop icon Christina Aguilera giving him VD and providing oral gratifica-tion to Limp Bizkit frontman Fred Durst and MTV VJ Carson Daly aroused the ire of the blond nineteen-year-old diva, who stated, through a spokesman, "It is disgusting and offensive and above all it's not true." She later commented to *MTV News*, "I don't know what I said to disturb him, but whatever I said, I'd say it again."

But Aguilera stopped short of threatening to sue Eminem because, she said, "suing for slander requires that somebody takes him seriously. It's obvious in the song that he's making this stuff up about a lot of people."

When asked by MTV's Kurt Loder about the Aguilera flap, Em allowed that the oral-sex claim "probably wasn't" true, and revealed that he had been offended when Aguilera speculated about his personal life on her MTV special *What a Girl Wants*.

"She heard a rumor that I was married, and then said, 'He's cute, but isn't he married, though?'" Eminem explained. "And then she said, 'Doesn't he have a song about killing his baby's mother?'... So I figured, 'All right, you said something about me, I'm gonna voice some rumors that I heard about you.'"

Aguilera wasn't the only celebrity on the receiving end of a verbal assault in "The Real Slim Shady." In the course of railing against his critics—and arguing that his lyrical content is no more salacious than what kids see every day on the Discovery Channel—Em makes reference to Pamela Anderson's allegedly violent relationship with Tommy Lee, and to MTV prankster Tom Green canoodling with "a dead moose."

"A lot of things I say are not meant to be disses, they're just meant to be me speaking my mind," Em notes. "If I wanna diss somebody, then I'll diss 'em; I'll just come out and say 'Will Smith, fuck him.' "

Indeed, one of the most prominent targets for Em's displeasure on "The Real Slim Shady" is rapper-turned-movie-star Smith, specifically his somewhat self-serving anti-profanity stance.

"I respect him for saying his opinion, but not everybody is as happy as Will Smith," Em commented. "So if he sees life [as being] about birds and bees and flowers, then let him rap about birds and bees and flowers, but don't diss nobody else . . . I felt like he was taking a stab at me and Dre and anybody who uses profanity on a record to express themselves."

The album gained further pre-release notoriety from a lyric on "I'm Back," in which Eminem denies having any sexual interest in Aguilera. He then states that he'd prefer to impregnate sexy actress/singer Jennifer Lopez, addressing apologies to her boyfriend, trouble-prone hip-hop entrepreneur Sean "Puff Daddy" Combs.

Responding to the track in typically grandiose fashion, Puffy issued a press release. "Eminem called me and explained," stated Combs. "We both understand this is hip-hop. It's entertainment, it's not personal and so I don't have a problem with it. Every man is entitled to fantasize . . . It is just a record, not a reality."

But some of the album's most barbed attacks were reserved for the vapid teen-pop acts with whom Eminem shared space in the upper reaches of the pop charts. "The whole pop world is corny," Em observed. "I just think it's sissy music. It's just so watered-down, man. It's like, how many times can you rhyme 'tearin' me apart' and 'breakin' my heart' and 'love, sent from up above.' It's ridiculous, it's repetitive, and it gets on my nerves."

Indeed, Eminem's new material seemed to spare no one—not even his mentor Dr.

Dre. In "The Real Slim Shady," Em even claims to have murdered Dre and locked his body in his basement. The song's video contains a shot of a milk carton with a photo of a distraught-looking Dre.

"He was cool with it, he laughed," Em told Kurt Loder. "I think I killed him two or three times on this record. I kill my girl, I kill Dre . . . I think I kill *you* on this album.

"On this album, I touched on every person that I didn't like. That's my way of venting, writing it down and getting back at people through words. Because I feel like I can use words as weapons against people."

The comically elaborate video for "The Real Slim Shady," co-directed by Dr. Dre, included a scene set at a faux Grammy show, with Eminem dolled up in Britney Spears drag, and cameos by Fred Durst and a life-size inflatable doll bearing a suspicious resemblance to Christina Aguilera. The video also features cameos by rappers Method Man and Redman, along with scenes of a roomful of Eminem lookalikes, a factory assembly line converting a procession of average Joes into Slim Shady clones, and a cartoonish mental-hospital dayroom where Em is attended by an annoyed-looking nurse played by actress/comedian Kathy Griffin.

"It was fun—I got to beat up Eminem," Griffin told *Time Out NY*. "I think the boy doesn't get beaten up enough, actually. He should hire someone to give him a little whack on the head every day . . . He just spent the whole day shouting about how he wanted to go home—you know, he's young and all."

Beginning in late April, Eminem debuted some of *The Marshall Mathers LP*'s material on tour. The Friday before the album's release, he performed at Long Island's Nassau Coliseum as the closing act of the Spring Break 2000 show, sharing the bill with Method Man, Redman, Rah Digga, Black Rob, Ginuwine, Nas, Canibus and Carl Thomas. Eminem closed the show with an hour-long set, clowning with a Christina Aguilera doll before performing "The Real Slim Shady."

That weekend, Eminem invaded MTV's Times Square studio to host "EmTV," a wacky two-hour variation on the channel's *Total Request Live*. Promising to show no videos by "The Wackstreet Boys," " 'N Stink" and "98 Disease," Em traded barbs with

Carson Daly, took phone calls from listeners and fielded questions from studio-audience members. He also assumed such alter egos as goofy would-be b-boy Raymond Munns and MTV news anchor Hurt Shoulder, did a convincing imitation of Oasis frontman Liam Gallagher and confronted a studio audience full of Eminem impersonators.

He also performed in elaborate spoofs of such MTV staples as *Undressed*, *Fanatic* (with an appearance by Funkmaster Flex), the karaoke competition *Say What* (as a goofy frat boy delivering a hapless rendition of "My Name Is") and *The Tom Green Show* (with Em, disguised as a whiny Green, accosting annoyed citizens on the streets of midtown Manhattan).

On Tuesday, the day that his new disc hit the streets, Eminem was a guest on the real *Total Request Live*. Later that day, Em celebrated the album's release with an appearance at the Virgin Megastore in Times Square. In contrast to the album's copious assortment of disses, Eminem was gracious and down-to-earth with his fans, hugging and kissing female admirers and bantering with male fans while autographing copies of the new album. Also in attendance were members of D-12, whose debut album was scheduled for release later in 2000. The store was packed with hundreds of fans, while hundreds more waited outside to catch a glimpse of the star. The loving vibe was broken briefly, when a wild-eyed fiftyish man brandishing a pen lunged toward the star before being dragged away by security guards.

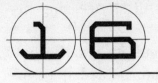

Any notion that Eminem's success was a one-shot fad vanished with *The Marshall Mathers LP*'s release. The album—on which Dr. Dre, who's credited as executive producer, splits production duties with FBT and Eminem himself—boasted a more aggressive, rock-influenced sound than its predecessor, with Em singing on several tracks.

Aside from its headline-grabbing celebrity disses, *The Marshall Mathers LP* presented a somewhat darker, more reality-based vibe than its predecessor, living up to the artist's promise that his

119

new material would more closely reflect his inner self while still showcasing his comedic verbal skills.

The album establishes its volatile balance of anger and humor immediately. After "Public Service Announcement 2000" concludes with Em inviting his enemies to sue him, "Kill You" finds him fantasizing about raping his mother, while gloating over his infiltration of the mainstream entertainment world and complaining about the controversy surrounding his fame.

But the mask of ultraviolent bravado drops on the next track, "Stan." Built around a sample of English chanteuse Dido's "Thank You," "Stan" offers a chilling yet oddly compassionate portrait of a desperate, disgruntled and ultimately violent Eminem fan. The story is told through a series of progressively hostile letters from Stan to his hero, culminating in the title character's tragically misguided copycat slaying of his pregnant girlfriend. The situation is portrayed with surprising empathy and insight, belying Em's prevailing image as an irresponsible smart-ass.

While "Stan" finds Eminem confronting

the question of his own responsibility for his fans' actions, on "Who Knew" and "The Way I Am," he angrily rejects the notion that he's a role model and rails against parents who blame him for their kids' behavior rather than addressing their own parenting skills. But his palpable anger over the controversy that surrounds him doesn't stop him from slipping tasteless references to the riding accident that paralyzed actor Christopher Reeve and the skiing mishap that killed Sonny Bono into "Who Knew."

After "Remember Me," which spotlights guest rappers RBX and Sticky Fingaz, Em is once again proudly proclaiming how unhinged he is on "I'm Back," revisiting his unhappy childhood and fantasizing about executing a lineup of bullies.

On the epic "Marshall Mathers," on which he sings an affectingly vulnerable-sounding chorus, Em again bemoans the complications from his new fame, and lets loose on the Backstreet Boys, Ricky Martin, 'N Sync, Britney Spears and even has-been pop icons Vanilla Ice and New Kids on the Block.

"Marshall Mathers" also makes reference to Eminem's battles with various relatives, including the still-unresolved lawsuit filed by his mother, which his lawyers advised him not to discuss in interviews. "It really pisses me off that I can't talk about it," he admitted at the time. "It gets under my skin a little bit that I can't say things and make comments, because I want to, but I'll just keep quiet right now because I'm paying out my ass for lawyers as it is."

"Marshall Mathers" is followed by a cheerfully filthy comic vignette which purports to depict Insane Clown Posse members Shaggy 2Dope and Violent J. performing oral sex on recurring character Ken Kaniff while fantasizing that he's really Eminem.

Things get serious again on the confessional "Drug Ballad," which features a return appearance by "Cum On Everybody" vocalist Dina Rae. Em explained that the song was inspired by his own experiences in the wake of *The Slim Shady LP*'s surprise success. "The last year was a really crazy year for me, so I don't think anybody saw me not drunk or not on some type of substance," he said. "Fame hit me so fast I didn't even know what I was doing.

"I didn't know how big my record was gonna be, and I didn't know if this opportunity was ever gonna come to me again, so it was like, I was doing each and every thing that I could do. Any chance to be on TV, any chance to do a show or promote the album, I was doing, and barely slept. So the drugs kept me alive, they kept me going . . . But I've learned to pace myself better this year."

The swaggering "Amityville" spotlights Em's pal Bizarre, while "Bitch Please II" is a steamy slice of gangsta rap that features Dr. Dre, Snoop Dogg, Xzibit and Nate Dogg and namechecks *Billboard* editor-in-chief and avowed Eminem adversary Timothy White. "Under the Influence" finds Em trading rhymes with fellow D-12 members Bizarre, Proof, Kuniva, Swifty and Kon Artis. And "Criminal" ends the album with Em robbing a bank and making a tasteless reference to fashion designer Gianni Versace, who was murdered by a gay gunman.

Though Eminem and Kim were now

married and living, seemingly happily, with their daughter in a newly purchased home, Em's embattled spouse didn't escape unscathed in her husband's new rhymes. One of *The Marshall Mathers LP*'s most memorable—and most chilling—tracks is "Kim," which purports to portray the violent argument that precipitated the murderous events of *The Slim Shady LP*'s " '97 Bonnie and Clyde." But unlike its outlandishly over-the-top predecessor, "Kim" is unnervingly real, offering an emotionally unsparing insight on Em's own insecurities and his and Kim's love/hate relationship.

The artist explained that "Kim" was inspired by one of the couple's periodic breakups. "We were seeing other people, and it upset me so bad that she was seeing somebody else that I just pictured her in my face, and me being able to scream at her and really tell her how I felt.

"When she first heard ' '97 Bonnie and Clyde,' she was like, 'You're an asshole.' . . .When [she first heard 'Kim'], we were both sitting in the car and she just looked over at me and I said, 'You have anything to say?' She was like 'You're fuckin' crazy. You're crazy.'

"I feel like I don't need therapy," he continued. "I feel like my music is my therapy. Because once I sit down and write, I get everything off my chest. People might think that I walk around mad all day, and I'm not. For the most part I'm happy. I get all my aggression out in the studio."

The album's alternating front-cover art presented Eminem as either a moody white-trash incarnate, sitting alone on the porch of a modest-looking house, or huddled in a dark alleyway. Inside the CD booklet, photos of Em as both a child and as a proud parent share space with posed shots of the artist as minimum-wage worker tossing garbage into a Dumpster.

According to Jeff Bass, Em himself (who receives production and/or mixing credit on seven of the album's tracks) had considerably more hands-on involvement in the production process this time around. "The first album, it was all kind of new to him," he said. "Now, if he wants to change something in the music, he'll hum something, and we'll interpret what he's humming.

"I think a lot of people are waiting for him to not do as well with this album, but he has something that's unique," Bass continued. "He is not just your average rapper. He really is true to the hip-hop game, and his skills are unreal. I don't think the sophomore jinx will affect him at all."

The critics seemed to notice the progress, while continuing to wrestle with the contradictions inherent in Eminem's complex persona. *Entertainment Weekly*'s Will Hermes even split the magazine's customary letter-grade rating system into three different grades, giving the album an A-plus for media savvy, D-plus for moral responsibility and A-minus for overall artistry.

Calling Eminem "a peerless poet with a profound understanding of the power of language," Hermes described the album as "indefensible and critic-proof, hypocritical and heartbreaking, unlistenable and undeniable; it's a disposable shock-rap session, and the first great pop record of the twenty-first century. It plays to a culture obsessed with celebrity gossip and talk-show voyeurism at the same time it rails against that culture.

"In the end," Hermes concluded, "it's impossible to separate the art from the ugliness, the hilarity from the viciousness, or the 'realness' from the calculation. *The Marshall Mathers LP* is a fun-house mirror held up to an artist's pain, anger and selfish ambition, as well as to the three-ring media circus in which we live."

Jim Farber, reviewing the album in New York's *Daily News*, noted that Eminem "tries as hard as possible to appall you with new tales of matricide, suicide, necrophilia, bestiality, drug abuse, stalking— every social horror short of public nose-picking. At the same time, he interjects reminders that only a moron would take his hyperbolic rants and potty-mouthed outbursts literally. Along the way, Eminem unearths, and exorcises, some genuine teen-boy anxieties and frustrations."

Elsewhere, Kurt Loder, in an editorial published in *MTV News Online*, noted, "Eminem brings you up short; he gets you laughing before you have time to take in the full awfulness of what it is he has you laughing at . . . *Marshall Mathers* has a razor-sharp and ferocious command of language, a level of verbal skill that, in another context, would qualify as poetic."

Eminem continued to deny that he

hated women or gays. " 'Faggot' to me doesn't necessarily mean gay people. 'Faggot' to me just means you're a sissy, you're a coward," he insisted. "When I started saying 'faggot' on record I started getting people going 'Do you have something against gay people?' and I thought it was funny, because I don't."

Still, it wasn't a huge surprise when the Gay and Lesbian Alliance Against Defamation issued a condemnation of *The Marshall Mathers LP* just days after its release. "Eminem's lyrics are soaked with violence and full of negative comments about many groups, including lesbians and gay men," the statement read. "Such disregard for others can lead to discrimination, physical abuse and even death." While GLAAD acknowledged Eminem's right to free speech, it also accused Interscope Records and its distributor, Universal, of irresponsibility in promoting the album to "adolescent males, the very group that statistically commits the most hate crimes."

Em—who stated that his commercial success had "opened a lot of doors for me to push the freedom of speech to the limit" with *The Marshall Mathers LP*—continued to stick to his guns. "I don't feel like I should have to bite my tongue for anybody. I really believe in freedom of speech, I can't stress that enough . . . I believe an artist should be an artist and be able to say whatever he wants to say, whether you think it's good or bad."

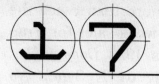

Condemnations and critical analyses aside, *The Marshall Mathers LP* was an instant smash, selling a remarkable 1.7 million in its first week of release—a week that also included such high-profile discs as Don Henley's *Inside Job*, Matchbox Twenty's *Mad Season* and A Perfect Circle's *Mer de Noms*.

The fact that he bounced Britney Spears' just-released second album *Oops!. . . I Did It Again* (which sold 1.3 million in its first week) from the top slot of the sales chart must have been a source of some satisfaction to Eminem. In addition, *The Marshall Mathers LP*'s first-week showing was more than twice the highest previous first-week sales for a rap album (Snoop Dogg's 1993 *Doggystyle*), and was second only to 'N Sync's *No Strings Attached*, as the fastest-selling album in the nine-year history of the music-industry sales-tracking company SoundScan.

Eminem spent much of the summer of 2000 back on the road, teaming with Dr. Dre, Dre's former N.W.A. partner Ice Cube, Dre's brother Warren G, and long-time Dre cohorts Snoop Dogg, Nate Dogg and Kurupt, along with Dre-associated up-and-comers Xzibit and Devin, for the much-touted six-week Up In Smoke Tour.

"It's gonna be unlike any hip-hop show out there," predicted Dr. Dre, and indeed Up In Smoke, in addition to being one of the biggest hip-hop tours in history, was also the most visually elaborate, with giant video screens showing short film vignettes and an elaborate stage set designed to look like an inner-city parking lot.

With lightning now having struck twice to prove him to be both a legitimate artist and a genuine cultural phenomenon, Eminem made it clear that his far-reaching success was unlikely to alter his uncompromising stance.

"I'm making a statement that I'm not gonna watch my mouth. I don't feel like I need to [think] 'Oh my gosh, should I write this? I don't know, this might offend somebody.' *I* been getting offended all my life.

"All I've done is take shit," he said. "Now I'm gonna start dishin' it out."